The 54-Day Rosary Novena

THE
54-DAY
ROSARY
NOVENA

Our Sunday Visitor
Huntington, Indiana

Nihil Obstat
Msgr. Michael Heintz, Ph.D.
Censor Librorum

Imprimatur
✠ Kevin C. Rhoades
Bishop of Fort Wayne-South Bend
April 7, 2025

The *Nihil Obstat* and *Imprimatur* are official declarations that a book is free from doctrinal or moral error. It is not implied that those who have granted the *Nihil Obstat* and *Imprimatur* agree with the contents, opinions, or statements expressed.

Our Sunday Visitor Publishing Division
Our Sunday Visitor, Inc.
200 Noll Plaza
Huntington, IN 46750
www.osv.com
1-800-348-2440

ISBN: 978-1-63966-366-8 (Inventory No. T2997)
1. RELIGION—Prayerbooks —Christian.
2. RELIGION—Christian Living—Prayer.
3. RELIGION—Christianity—Catholic.

LCCN: 2025913756

Cover and interior design: Chelsea Alt
Cover and interior art: Adobe Stock

PRINTED IN THE UNITED STATES OF AMERICA

Contents

What Is the 54-Day Rosary Novena?

The 54-Day Rosary Novena dates back to 1884, when Our Lady appeared to Fortuna Agrelli, a young girl enduring great physical suffering. Her family had recently completed a novena of rosaries in petition for her healing. A few days later, Fortuna was favored with an apparition of the Blessed Mother, who appeared with the Infant Jesus and Saints Dominic and Catherine of Siena.

Mary encouraged the girl to pray three novenas in petition, promising that she would obtain all she had requested in prayer. Then she also told her to pray three novenas in thanksgiving. Fortuna received a miraculous healing, and devotion to the 54-Day Rosary Novena began to spread.

The 54-Day Rosary Novena actually includes six full novenas of nine days each. The first three novenas are prayed in petition for a particular cause or need, and the final three in thanksgiving for prayers answered, even if our prayers have not yet been answered by the time we begin the last three novenas. This novena requires our trust that God does indeed hear our prayers and will answer them according to his will, and in his good time.

Praying the novenas in sets of three also brings to mind the Trinity: Father, Son, and Holy Spirit.

The Rosary begins with the First Joyful Mystery (the Annunciation). This mystery sets the tone for the whole 54-Day Rosary Novena because it focuses on Mary's willingness to accept God's will for her life. As we pray and meditate on all the mysteries of the Rosary in the weeks ahead, we will strive to both accept and be grateful for the way the Lord will answer our prayers — whether that answer is yes, no, or not yet.

●·····●·····●·····●·····●·····●

How Is a 54-Day Rosary Novena Different from the Daily Practice of Praying the Rosary?

Many people pray the Rosary on a daily basis, but that prayer practice differs from the 54-Day Rosary Novena in a few significant ways.

First, when praying the daily Rosary, we might dedicate particular days of the week to pray for certain intentions. For example, we might pray for our deceased loved ones on Tuesdays or Fridays, the days on which the Sorrowful Mysteries are traditionally prayed. However, when praying a 54-Day Rosary Novena, we pray the Joyful Mysteries on the first day of the novena, no matter what day of the week it is. On the second day, we pray the Luminous Mysteries, the Sorrowful Mysteries on the third day, and the Glorious Mysteries on the fourth. On the fifth day, we'll begin again with the Joyful Mysteries. Later in this book, you'll find a tracker to help you remember which mysteries to pray on any given day.

The 54-Day Rosary Novena is prayed for a singular intention that will not vary according to the day of the week or the mysteries prayed. You will pray the Rosary for that intention or need every day for fifty-four days: the first twenty-seven in petition and the next twenty-seven in thanksgiving. Praying the 54-Day Rosary Novena will require perseverance, and during this novena, we will ask the Blessed Mother to help us grow in hope, perseverance, patience, gratitude, and faith as we approach her daily in prayer.

In the Hail Mary, which we pray fifty-three times with each Rosary, we implore the Blessed Mother to "pray for us sinners, now and at the hour of our death." Mary cannot grant our requests herself, but she can — and we believe she does — bring them to God through her prayers. Mary intercedes for us in heaven in the same way we intercede for our loved ones by praying for them.

Whenever we pray the Rosary, we are meditating on the life of Christ. The mysteries of the Rosary offer us opportunities to ponder the major events in Christ's life through the eyes of the Blessed Virgin Mary, who always leads us to her son.

When we pray the 54-Day Rosary Novena, we heed Saint Paul, who reminds us to confidently place our intentions in God's hands, knowing that our every prayer is heard: "Have no anxiety at all, but in everything, by prayer and petition, with thanksgiving, make your requests known to God" (Phil 4:6).

● · · · · · ● · · · · · ● · · · · · ● · · · · · ● · · · · · ●

Our Prayers Never Go Unanswered

As we can learn from the Bible and from the lives of many saints, prayers — even very fervent prayers — are not always answered immediately or in the way we hope. For example, Saint Monica prayed for almost twenty years for the conversion of her son and husband. Eventually, those conversions did happen. Anna the Prophetess prayed for several decades in the Temple and finally was able to announce that the redemption of Israel was at hand when she encountered Jesus at the Presentation (see Lk 2:36–38).

In the Gospel of Matthew, Jesus makes it clear that God does "give good things to those who ask him" (Mt 7:11). When we pray, we trust that God hears us and that we will be answered; this is why the 54-Day Rosary Novena has two components: petition and thanksgiving. We cannot force God to give us what we want when we want it, whether through a 54-Day Rosary Novena or any other promise we might make or prayer we might pray. Jesus let us know that God will give us what is good for us — but that might not always be what we expect or at the time we expect it.

Blessed Solanus Casey famously said, "Thank God ahead of time," and that statement underscores the confidence we'll bring as we approach God in praying our 54-Day Rosary Novena, particularly during the second half of the novena which focuses on thanksgiving. Even if we can't see how God is working to answer our prayers, we know that, in his goodness and generosity, he wants what is best for his people, and our pleas will not go unheard.

●·····●·····●·····●·····●·····●

Planning to Pray the 54-Day Rosary Novena

Use this tracker to help you remember which mystery to pray on which date.

J	L	S	G	J	L	S	G	J
__	__	__	__	__	__	__	__	__
J	L	S	G	J	L	S	G	J
__	__	__	__	__	__	__	__	__
J	L	S	G	J	L	S	G	J
__	__	__	__	__	__	__	__	__
J	L	S	G	J	L	S	G	J
__	__	__	__	__	__	__	__	__
J	L	S	G	J	L	S	G	J
__	__	__	__	__	__	__	__	__
J	L	S	G	J	L	S	G	J
__	__	__	__	__	__	__	__	__

You may wish to tie your 54-Day Rosary Novena to a Marian feast day or, if you are praying about an urgent situation, you can begin your prayers at any time. You are not required to begin or end your novena on a Marian feast, but for an ongoing need, this is a lovely way to honor a special devotion to the Blessed Mother.

If you would like to schedule your 54-Day Rosary Novena to end on a Marian feast day, use the START DATE column in the table below to find the next date on which to begin praying the Novena so you'll end on a Marian feast. Or, if you prefer, you can use the DATE column to select a Marian feast day on which to begin the Novena. It's up to you!

DATE	FEAST	START DATE
January 1	Solemnity of Mary, Mother of God	November 9
February 2	The Presentation of the Lord	December 11
February 11	Our Lady of Lourdes	December 20
March 25	The Annunciation of the Lord	January 31
May 13	Our Lady of Fatima	March 21
May 31	The Visitation	April 8

June 27	Our Lady of Perpetual Help	May 5
July 16	Our Lady of Mount Carmel	May 24
August 15	The Assumption of the Blessed Virgin Mary	June 23
August 22	The Queenship of the Blessed Virgin Mary	June 30
September 8	The Birth of Mary	July 16
September 15	Our Lady of Sorrows	July 24
October 7	Our Lady of the Rosary	August 15
November 21	The Presentation of the Blessed Virgin Mary	September 29
November 28	Our Lady of Kibeho	October 6
December 8	The Immaculate Conception of the Blessed Virgin Mary	October 16
December 10	Our Lady of Loreto	October 18
December 12	Our Lady of Guadalupe	October 20

As you pray the Rosary, you walk with the Blessed Mother through some of the most significant moments in her life and the life of Christ. Before praying the mysteries of the Rosary, follow the Virgin Mary's example of pondering these things in her heart. Pope St. Paul VI reminds us in *Marialis Cultus*: "By its nature the recitation of the Rosary calls for a quiet rhythm and a lingering pace, helping the individual to meditate on the mysteries of the Lord's life as seen through the eyes of her who was closest to the Lord. In this way the unfathomable riches of these mysteries are unfolded" (47).

Bring to mind your special intention for this 54-Day Rosary Novena and ask the Blessed Mother to pray for and with you as you offer your prayers each day.

Praying the 54-Day Rosary Novena

Are you new to praying the Rosary, or do you need a refresher course on the prayers? You'll find the prayers you need to get started in the section titled "How to Pray the Rosary" at the end of this book.

Remember that we are trusting God with the intention behind our prayers. With every "Thy will be done" we pray and every mystery we contemplate, we allow God to work in our hearts, building our trust in him day by day as we pray this novena.

Begin each day with the Daily Opening Prayer (below). Then continue to the set of mysteries for the day, which includes an opening prayer for the mysteries, a concluding prayer at the end of each decade, and a closing prayer of spiritual communion.

● ⋯⋯● ⋯⋯● ⋯⋯● ⋯⋯● ⋯⋯●

Daily Opening Prayer

O Jesus, at the moment of your death on the cross, you gave Mary to us as our mother, who continually points us toward you. Through this Rosary Novena, I pray for the grace to accept your will and to grow closer to your mother and to you.

Through Mary's intercession, I come before you today to ask this favor:

_____

_____

_____

_____

_____

_____

_____

_____

Lord Jesus Christ, hear the prayers I humbly bring before you on this day. Help me, today and every day, to persevere in prayer as I seek to know and accept your will. Amen.

PRAYERS IN PETITION

Claude Mellan, *Annunciation*, 1666, The Met Museum,
Harris Brisbane Dick Fund, 1953

The Joyful Mysteries

Rejoice in hope, endure in affliction,
persevere in prayer.

— Romans 12:12

As we pray the Joyful Mysteries of the Rosary in petition for this special intention, we ponder each mystery with a focus on strengthening our hope. We need to hang on to hope when facing difficult circumstances and situations, and hope motivates us to persevere in prayer.

Opening Prayer for the
Joyful Mysteries
(in Petition)

Hail, Queen of the Most Holy Rosary, my Mother Mary, hail! At your feet I humbly kneel to offer you a crown of roses, snow white buds to remind you of your joys, each bud recalling to you a holy mystery, each ten bound together with my petition for a particular grace. O Holy Queen, dispenser of God's graces, and mother of all who invoke you! You cannot look upon my gift and fail to see its binding. As you receive my gift, so will you receive my petition; from your bounty you will give me the favor I so earnestly and trustingly seek. I despair of nothing that I ask of you. Show yourself my mother!

_____

_____

_____

_____

_____

_____

_____

The First Joyful Mystery: The Annunciation

Mary said, "Behold, I am the handmaid of the Lord. May it be done to me according to your word." Then the angel departed from her.

— Luke 1:38

Mary, you received the message of the Archangel Gabriel and did not hesitate to say yes to God's plan, even when you didn't fully understand. You obediently took on your role as the mother of Christ, who would bring hope to the world. While you were sinless, that doesn't mean your life was easy. Accepting God's will is not always easy. I come to you in hope today, praying that I, too, can learn to accept God's will without arguing, complaining, or resisting.

Mary, Queen of the Most Holy Rosary, pray for me. Help me to grow in hope and to accept the will of God in this and in all things. Amen.

●·····●·····●·····●·····●·····●

Concluding Prayer: I bind these snow-white buds with a petition for the virtue of humility and humbly lay this bouquet at your feet.

The Second Joyful Mystery:
The Visitation

Blessed are you who believed that what was spoken to
you by the Lord would be fulfilled.

— Luke 1:45

Mary, through the Holy Spirit, your cousin Elizabeth was the first to recognize the fruits of your deep faith and the first to rejoice that, through your obedience to God, hope would finally come into the world. I come to you in hope today, praying that the Holy Spirit will help me recognize, like Elizabeth did, that God continues to accomplish his will in the world.

Mary, Queen of the Most Holy Rosary, pray for me. Help me to grow in hope and to accept the will of God in this and in all things. Amen.

●·····●·····●·····●·····●·····●

Concluding Prayer: I bind these snow-white buds with a petition for the virtue of charity and humbly lay this bouquet at your feet.

The Third Joyful Mystery:
The Birth of Our Lord

The angel said to them, "Do not be afraid; for behold, I proclaim to you good news of great joy that will be for all the people. For today in the city of David a savior has been born for you who is Messiah and Lord."

— *Luke 2:10–11*

The Savior, long-awaited and hoped for by all of God's people, has been born — in unexpected and humble circumstances. When the angel announced the fulfillment of that hope to the shepherds as they kept watch, they did not hesitate but rushed to the stable to see the newborn King. Like the shepherds who were the first to honor Jesus, I humbly come to you, Mary, holding to the hope that my prayer will be granted and that I will rejoice in seeing God's promises fulfilled.

Mary, Queen of the Most Holy Rosary, pray for me. Help me to grow in hope and to accept the will of God in this and in all things. Amen.

●⸳⸳⸳⸳●⸳⸳⸳⸳●⸳⸳⸳⸳●⸳⸳⸳⸳●⸳⸳⸳⸳●

Concluding Prayer: I bind these snow-white buds with a petition for the virtue of detachment from the world and humbly lay this bouquet at your feet.

The Fourth Joyful Mystery:
The Presentation in the Temple

Now, Master, you may let your servant go
in peace, according to your word,
for my eyes have seen your salvation,
which you prepared in sight of all the peoples,
a light for revelation to the Gentiles,
and glory for your people Israel.

— *Luke 2:29–32*

Simeon embodied the hope of God's people. In Luke 2:26 we read the Holy Spirit had revealed to Simeon he would live to see the Messiah. In this mystery, we celebrate the fulfillment of that hope. Simeon knew, without being told, that the infant brought to the Temple that day by Mary and Joseph was the Savior. Mary, I come to you in hope today. Help me to stay open to the Holy Spirit and see the way God is working in my life.

Mary, Queen of the Most Holy Rosary, pray for me. Help me to grow in hope and to accept the will of God in this and in all things. Amen.

● · · · · ● · · · · · ● · · · · · ● · · · · · ● · · · · · ●

Concluding Prayer: I bind these snow-white buds with a petition for the virtue of purity and humbly lay this bouquet at your feet.

The Fifth Joyful Mystery: The Finding of the Child Jesus in the Temple

After three days they found him in the temple, sitting in the midst of the teachers, listening to them and asking them questions, and all who heard him were astounded at his understanding and his answers.
— Luke 2:46–47

Mary, your agony and distress over the disappearance of your son reassures me that you understand the anxieties I feel. You did not give up searching for Jesus until you found him, and I am resolved to persevere in my prayer. I come to you in hope today. Help me to remain strong in faith, trust, and hope.

Mary, Queen of the Most Holy Rosary, pray for me. Help me to grow in hope and to accept the will of God in this and in all things. Amen.

•·····•·····•·····•·····•·····•

Concluding Prayer: I bind these snow-white buds with a petition for the virtue of obedience and humbly lay this bouquet at your feet.

Closing Prayer for the Joyful Mysteries
(in Petition)

Spiritual Communion: My Jesus, I believe that you are present in the most Blessed Sacrament. I love you above all things and I desire to receive you into my soul. Since I cannot now receive you sacramentally, come at least spiritually into my heart. I embrace you as if you were already there and unite myself wholly to you. Never permit me to be separated from you. Amen.

•·····•·····•·····•·····•·····•

Concluding Prayer: Sweet Mother Mary, I offer you this spiritual communion to bind my bouquets in a wreath to place upon your brow. O my mother! Look with favor upon my gift, and in your love obtain for me my request. Amen.

Paul Gleditsch, *The Baptism of Christ; Saint John the Baptist at right and Christ at left with his hands held together, the Holy Dove above, angels in the background, after Reni*, ca. 1815–72, The Metropolitan Museum of Art, Harris Brisbane Dick Fund, 1947

The Luminous Mysteries

You need endurance to do the will of God
and receive what he has promised.

— Hebrews 10:36

As we pray the Luminous Mysteries of the Rosary in petition for this special intention, we ponder each mystery with a focus on perseverance. We seek the strength to remain in hope and endure in our prayers.

Opening Prayer for the
Luminous Mysteries
(in Petition)

Hail, Queen of the Most Holy Rosary, my Mother Mary, hail! At your feet I humbly kneel to offer you a crown of roses, bright yellow buds to remind you of the ministry of your son, each bud recalling to you a holy mystery, each ten bound together with my petition for a particular grace. O Holy Queen, dispenser of God's graces, and mother of all who invoke you! You cannot look upon my gift and fail to see its binding. As you receive my gift, so will you receive my petition; from your bounty you will give me the favor I so earnestly and trustingly seek. I despair of nothing that I ask of you. Show yourself my mother!

_____

_____

_____

_____

_____

_____

The First Luminous Mystery:
The Baptism in the Jordan

After Jesus was baptized, he came up from the water and behold, the heavens were opened [for him], and he saw the Spirit of God descending like a dove [and] coming upon him. And a voice came from the heavens, saying, "This is my beloved Son, with whom I am well pleased."
— *Matthew 3:16–17*

The events of Jesus' baptism clearly point to his place in the Trinity and his role in carrying out the will of God. Mary, I come to you today, seeking the strength to persevere in seeking God's will in all things. Help me to trust that I can know and follow God's will.

Mary, Queen of the Most Holy Rosary, pray for me. Help me to grow in perseverance and to accept the will of God in this and in all things. Amen.

⚫ ⋯⋯ ⚫ ⋯⋯ ⚫ ⋯⋯ ⚫ ⋯⋯ ⚫ ⋯⋯ ⚫

Concluding Prayer: I bind these bright yellow roses with a petition for the grace of openness to the Holy Spirit and humbly lay this bouquet at your feet.

The Second Luminous Mystery:
The Wedding at Cana

*When the wine ran short, the mother of
Jesus said to him, "They have no wine."*
— John 2:3

Mary, when you approached Jesus to let him know
the problem the bridal couple at Cana was experiencing, you taught a great lesson in trust. You didn't tell
him how to fix the problem, but placed your concerns in
his hands and trusted that God's will would bring good
in a difficult situation. I come to you, praying that I, too,
will persevere in trusting God.

Mary, Queen of the Most Holy Rosary, pray for me.
Help me to grow in perseverance and to accept the will
of God in this and in all things. Amen.

Concluding Prayer: I bind these bright yellow roses with a
petition for the grace of manifestation through faith and
humbly lay this bouquet at your feet.

The Third Luminous Mystery:
The Proclamation of the Kingdom of God

*Jesus came to Galilee proclaiming the gospel of God:
"This is the time of fulfillment. The kingdom of
God is at hand. Repent, and believe in the gospel."*
— *Mark 1:14–15*

Repentance is not easy, but Jesus makes it clear that repentance is necessary. Mary, I come to you, knowing that while you had no need of repentance, you still endured many difficulties throughout your life. I pray that I will imitate your perseverance and always turn toward the Lord in my thoughts, words, and actions.

Mary, Queen of the Most Holy Rosary, pray for me. Help me to grow in perseverance and to accept the will of God in this and in all things. Amen.

•·····•·····•·····•·····•·····•

Concluding Prayer: I bind these bright yellow roses with a petition for the grace of trust in God and humbly lay this bouquet at your feet.

The Fourth Luminous Mystery:
The Transfiguration

Then from the cloud came a voice that said,
"This is my chosen Son; listen to him."
— *Luke 9:35*

All the noise and distractions of the world make listening to Jesus more challenging. Jesus took Peter, James, and John to a deserted place to give them a sense of his glory and to make sure they understood how necessary it was to listen to him. Mary, help me to follow your example and persevere in finding ways to listen for God and follow his will for me.

Mary, Queen of the Most Holy Rosary, pray for me. Help me to grow in perseverance and to accept the will of God in this and in all things. Amen.

●·····●·····●·····●·····●·····●

Concluding Prayer: I bind these bright yellow roses with a petition for the grace of desire for holiness and humbly lay this bouquet at your feet.

The Fifth Luminous Mystery:
The Institution of the Eucharist

*He took the bread, said the blessing, broke it, and
gave it to them, saying, "This is my body, which will
be given for you; do this in memory of me."*
— *Luke 22:19*

Jesus gave us his body in the Eucharist to strengthen
us in our journey of faith. He gave his life to give us
life eternal. Persevering in faith requires sacrifice. Mary,
I come to you today knowing the sacrifices you made
as the mother of God; you understand what it takes to
persevere.

Mary, Queen of the Most Holy Rosary, pray for me.
Help me to grow in perseverance and to accept the will
of God in this and in all things. Amen.

●·····●·····●·····●·····●·····●

Concluding Prayer: I bind these bright yellow roses with a
petition for the grace of adoration of the Eucharist and
humbly lay this bouquet at your feet.

Closing Prayer for the
Luminous Mysteries
(in Petition)

Spiritual Communion: My Jesus, I believe that you are present in the most Blessed Sacrament. I love you above all things and I desire to receive you into my soul. Since I cannot now receive you sacramentally, come at least spiritually into my heart. I embrace you as if you were already there and unite myself wholly to you. Never permit me to be separated from you. Amen.

●・・・・・●・・・・・●・・・・・●・・・・・●・・・・・●

Concluding Prayer: Sweet Mother Mary, I offer you this spiritual communion to bind my bouquets in a wreath to place upon your brow. O my mother! Look with favor upon my gift, and in your love obtain for me my request.

Benoit Thiboust, *Agony in the Garden*, 1680–1719, The Metropolita Museum of
Art, The Elisha Whittelsey Collection, The Elisha Whittelsey Fund, 1951

The Sorrowful Mysteries

*Put on then, as God's chosen ones, holy and
beloved, heartfelt compassion, kindness,
humility, gentleness, and patience.*

— *Colossians 3:12*

As we pray the Sorrowful Mysteries of the Rosary in petition for this special intention, we ponder each mystery with a focus on increasing our patience. It is difficult to wait for the Lord to answer our prayers; we pray that we will not lose heart, but that we will remain steadfast in prayer.

Opening Prayer for the Sorrowful Mysteries (in Petition)

Hail, Queen of the Most Holy Rosary, my Mother Mary, hail! At your feet I humbly kneel to offer you a crown of roses, blood-red roses to remind you of the passion of your divine son, with whom you fully partook of its bitterness, each rose recalling to you a holy mystery, each ten bound together with my petition for a particular grace. O Holy Queen, dispenser of God's graces, and mother of all who invoke you! You cannot look upon my gift and fail to see its binding. As you receive my gift, so will you receive my petition; from your bounty you will give me the favor I so earnestly and trustingly seek. I despair of nothing that I ask of you. Show yourself my mother!

_____

_____

_____

_____

_____

The First Sorrowful Mystery: The Agony in the Garden

When he returned he found them asleep. He said to Peter, "Simon, are you asleep? Could you not keep watch for one hour? Watch and pray that you may not undergo the test. The spirit is willing but the flesh is weak."

— *Mark 14:37–38*

As Jesus prayed in Gethsemane, the apostles abandoned him: first by falling asleep instead of praying beside him, and a little later by denying him and running away. Surely that added even more to Christ's agony. Mary, I pray for the patience to stay the course, not deserting Jesus when my prayer has not been answered, but waiting in hope for the Lord to hear my prayer.

Mary, Queen of the Most Holy Rosary, pray for me. Help me to grow in patience and to accept the will of God in this and in all things. Amen.

● · · · · · ● · · · · · ● · · · · · ● · · · · · ● · · · · · ●

Concluding Prayer: I bind these blood-red roses with a petition for the virtue of resignation to the will of God and humbly lay this bouquet at your feet.

The Second Sorrowful Mystery:
The Scourging at the Pillar

Then Pilate took Jesus and had him scourged.
— John 19:1

After enduring the agony in the garden and capture by the Roman soldiers, Jesus was physically tortured by order of Pontius Pilate, yet he did not give in to despair. When I pray but an answer does not come quickly, the temptation to despair can be great. Mary, I come to you to ask you to intercede for me, praying that I will remember that God answers all prayers in his own time.

Mary, Queen of the Most Holy Rosary, pray for me. Help me to grow in patience and to accept the will of God in this and in all things. Amen.

●·····●·····●·····●·····●·····●

Concluding Prayer: I bind these blood-red roses with a petition for the virtue of mortification and humbly lay this bouquet at your feet.

The Third Sorrowful Mystery:
The Crowning with Thorns

*They clothed him in purple and, weaving a
crown of thorns, placed it on him. They began
to salute him with, "Hail, King of the Jews!" and
kept striking his head with a reed and spitting
upon him. They knelt before him in homage.*

— *Mark 15:17–19*

Jesus was subjected not only to physical torture but to public humiliation as well. Mocking him, the soldiers echoed the shouts of the people who had greeted him at the entrance to the city only days before. Yet Jesus did not fight back; he stood fast, waiting patiently for the moment to pass. Mary, as I ponder the patience your son showed while the soldiers and bystanders taunted him, I pray that I, too, will have the patience and hope to endure the challenges I face.

Mary, Queen of the Most Holy Rosary, pray for me. Help me to grow in patience and to accept the will of God in this and in all things. Amen.

•·····•·····•·····•·····•·····•

Concluding Prayer: I bind these blood-red roses with a petition for the virtue of humility and humbly lay this bouquet at your feet.

The Fourth Sorrowful Mystery:
The Carrying of the Cross

*So they took Jesus, and carrying the cross
himself he went out to what is called the
Place of the Skull, in Hebrew, Golgotha.*
— *John 19:16–17*

Surely Jesus was exhausted by the time he was sent to drag the cross to the place of his death. He must have felt as if he had no strength left. Mary, you had to watch as your son carried his own cross; your strength and patience in suffering was greatly tested. I pray for the patience and strength I need to face this challenge.

Mary, Queen of the Most Holy Rosary, pray for me. Help me to grow in patience and to accept the will of God in this and in all things. Amen.

•·····•·····•·····•·····•·····•

Concluding Prayer: I bind these blood-red roses with a petition for the virtue of patience in adversity and humbly lay this bouquet at your feet.

The Fifth Sorrowful Mystery:
The Crucifixion

*Then they crucified him and divided his garments
by casting lots for them to see what each should
take. … Those passing by reviled him. … Jesus
gave a loud cry and breathed his last.*

— Mark 15:24–37

Mary, as your son suffered those final indignities and then died, you endured the unimaginable along with him. I look to your example as I, too, endure a trial; stand with me today and always as a model of motherly patience and strength.

Mary, Queen of the Most Holy Rosary, pray for me. Help me to grow in patience and to accept the will of God in this and in all things. Amen.

●·····●·····●·····●·····●·····●

Concluding Prayer: I bind these blood-red roses with a petition for the virtue of love of our enemies and humbly lay this bouquet at your feet.

Closing Prayer for the
Sorrowful Mysteries
(in Petition)

Spiritual Communion: My Jesus, I believe that you are present in the most Blessed Sacrament. I love you above all things and I desire to receive you into my soul. Since I cannot now receive you sacramentally, come at least spiritually into my heart. I embrace you as if you were already there and unite myself wholly to you. Never permit me to be separated from you. Amen.

* * * * *

Concluding Prayer: Sweet Mother Mary, I offer you this spiritual communion to bind my bouquets in a wreath to place upon your brow. O my mother! Look with favor upon my gift, and in your love obtain for me my request.

Follower of Francesco Fontebasso, *The Resurrection*, 18th century,
National Gallery of Art, Gift of Dr. and Mrs. Malcolm W. Bick

The Glorious Mysteries

Trust in the LORD with all your heart,
on your own intelligence do not rely;
In all your ways be mindful of him,
and he will make straight your paths.
— Proverbs 3:5–6

As we pray the Glorious Mysteries of the Rosary in petition for this special intention, we ponder each mystery with a focus on trust. These mysteries celebrate God's triumph over evil and sin, and in celebrating this triumph, we reaffirm that we can always trust God to keep his promises.

Opening Prayer for
the Glorious Mysteries
(in Petition)

Hail, Queen of the Most Holy Rosary, my Mother Mary, hail! At your feet I humbly kneel to offer you a crown of roses, full-blown white roses, tinged with the red of the passion, to remind you of your glories, fruits of the sufferings of your son and you, each rose recalling to you a holy mystery, each ten bound together with my petition for a particular grace. O Holy Queen, dispenser of God's graces, and mother of all who invoke you! You cannot look upon my gift and fail to see its binding. As you receive my gift, so will you receive my petition; from your bounty you will give me the favor I so earnestly and trustingly seek. I despair of nothing that I ask of you. Show yourself my mother!

_____

_____

_____

_____

_____

The First Glorious Mystery:
The Resurrection

"Why do you seek the living one among the dead? He is not here, but he has been raised. Remember what he said to you while he was still in Galilee, that the Son of Man must be handed over to sinners and be crucified, and rise on the third day." And they remembered his words.

— Luke 24:5–8

The women who returned to the tomb early that morning, intending to complete the burial rituals for Jesus, encountered the unexpected: an empty tomb and two angels, who reminded them that God had done as he said he would. Mary, you put your trust in God in every way, and your example reminds me that I am called to do likewise.

Mary, Queen of the Most Holy Rosary, pray for me. Help me to grow in trust and to accept the will of God in this and in all things. Amen.

•······•······•······•······•······•

Concluding Prayer: I bind these full-blown roses with a petition for the virtue of faith and humbly lay this bouquet at your feet.

The Second Glorious Mystery:
The Ascension of Our Lord

*Then he led them [out] as far as Bethany, raised
his hands, and blessed them. As he blessed them he
parted from them and was taken up to heaven.*
— *Luke 24:50–51*

Only a short while after Jesus' Resurrection, he was
miraculously taken up to heaven — and this time,
no one knew when he would return. They did know,
however, of his promise to return, and they trusted that
God would continue to fulfill his promises, as he had
done before. Mary, you saw firsthand how God fulfilled
those promises. Stand with me today as I strive to trust
God more, even in times of doubt and trial.

Mary, Queen of the Most Holy Rosary, pray for me.
Help me to grow in trust and to accept the will of God
in this and in all things. Amen.

●·····●·····●·····●·····●·····●

Concluding Prayer: I bind these full-blown roses with a
petition for the virtue of hope and humbly lay this bouquet at your feet.

The Third Glorious Mystery:
The Descent of the Holy Spirit

Peter [said] to them, "Repent and be baptized, every one of you, in the name of Jesus Christ for the forgiveness of your sins; and you will receive the gift of the holy Spirit. For the promise is made to you and to your children and to all those far off, whomever the Lord our God will call."
— *Acts 2:38–39*

When the Holy Spirit descended upon the apostles, Peter explained to everyone who had gathered around that this was the fulfillment of the promises of God. His trust and witness led to the conversion of many people. Mary, you saw the transformation of life that took place through the Holy Spirit. I, too, want to be transformed. Teach me to follow your example of openness to the Spirit and trust in God.

Mary, Queen of the Most Holy Rosary, pray for me. Help me to grow in trust and to accept the will of God in this and in all things. Amen.

• •

Concluding Prayer: I bind these full-blown roses with a petition for the virtue of charity and humbly lay this bouquet at your feet.

The Fourth Glorious Mystery:
The Assumption of Our Lady into Heaven

Taken up to heaven she did not lay aside this salvific duty, but by her constant intercession continued to bring us the gifts of eternal salvation.
— *Lumen Gentium, 62*

Mary, our Tradition reminds us that you continue to pray with us and for us in heaven. You know Jesus and are close to him in a way no other human person could ever be. Though you have left this world, you do not neglect the children who call to you. I pray that I will always trust you to pray for me, even as I learn to trust God in times of need.

Mary, Queen of the Most Holy Rosary, pray for me. Help me to grow in trust and to accept the will of God in this and in all things. Amen.

●······●······●······●······●······●

Concluding Prayer: I bind these full-blown roses with a petition for the virtue of union with Christ and humbly lay this bouquet at your feet.

The Fifth Glorious Mystery:
The Coronation of the Blessed Virgin Mary

*A great sign appeared in the sky, a woman clothed
with the sun, with the moon under her feet,
and on her head a crown of twelve stars.*

— Revelation 12:1

Mary, you are the queen of heaven. You will spend eternity in heaven as a reward for your trust in God. I look to you as a model of trust, and I hope my own trust in God will increase as I continue to pray and ponder your example.

Mary, Queen of the Most Holy Rosary, pray for me. Help me to grow in trust and to accept the will of God in this and in all things. Amen.

•·····•·····•·····•·····•·····•

Concluding Prayer: I bind these full-blown roses with a petition for the virtue of union with you and humbly lay this bouquet at your feet.

Closing Prayer for the
Sorrowful Mysteries
(in Petition)

Spiritual Communion: My Jesus, I believe that you are present in the most Blessed Sacrament. I love you above all things and I desire to receive you into my soul. Since I cannot now receive you sacramentally, come at least spiritually into my heart. I embrace you as if you were already there and unite myself wholly to you. Never permit me to be separated from you. Amen.

● ⋯⋯ ● ⋯⋯ ● ⋯⋯ ● ⋯⋯ ● ⋯⋯ ●

Concluding Prayer: Sweet Mother Mary, I offer you this spiritual communion to bind my bouquets in a wreath to place upon your brow. O my mother! Look with favor upon my gift, and in your love obtain for me my request.

PRAYERS IN THANKSGIVING

Nicolas Mignard, *The Visitation*, c. 1649, The Metropolit Museum of Art,
Gift of Matthieu de Bayser, 2010

The Joyful Mysteries

Amen, amen, I say to you, whatever you ask the Father in my name he will give you. Until now you have not asked anything in my name; ask and you will receive, so that your joy may be complete.
                                                    — *John 16:23–24*

As we pray the Joyful Mysteries of the Rosary in thanksgiving that the Lord hears our prayers for this special intention, we ponder each mystery with a focus on joy. We do not wait to rejoice and give thanks that our prayers are heard, because we are confident in the promises of God.

Opening Prayer for
the Joyful Mysteries
(in Thanksgiving)

Hail, Queen of the Most Holy Rosary, my Mother Mary, hail! At your feet I humbly kneel to offer you a crown of roses, snow white buds to remind you of your joys, each bud recalling to you a holy mystery, each ten bound together with my petition for a particular grace. O Holy Queen, dispenser of God's graces, and mother of all who invoke you! You cannot look upon my gift and fail to see its binding. As you receive my gift, so will you receive my thanksgiving; from your bounty, you have given me the favor I so earnestly and trustingly sought. I did not despair of what I asked of you, and you have truly shown yourself my mother.

_____

_____

_____

_____

_____

_____

The First Joyful Mystery:
The Annunciation

*And the Word became flesh and made his dwelling
among us, and we saw his glory, the glory as of
the Father's only Son, full of grace and truth.*
                                        — John 1:14

With the Annunciation and your "yes" to God, Mary, the glory of God came into the world. We rejoice in gratitude for what you allowed to happen when you accepted God's will for your life, and for God's gift of his Son to the world.

Mary, Queen of the Most Holy Rosary, pray for me. Help me to grow in joy and to accept the will of God in this and in all things. Amen.

●‧‧‧‧‧●‧‧‧‧‧●‧‧‧‧‧●‧‧‧‧‧●‧‧‧‧‧●

Concluding Prayer: I bind these snow-white buds with a petition for the virtue of humility and humbly lay this bouquet at your feet.

The Second Joyful Mystery:
The Visitation

*Blessed are you who believed that what was
spoken to you by the Lord would be fulfilled.*
— *Luke 1:45*

Elizabeth, filled with the joy that comes from trust in God's goodness, was the first to recognize that you were the mother of the long-awaited Messiah, Mary. She also affirmed the importance of your belief in God's promises and your willingness to do what God asked of you.

Mary, Queen of the Most Holy Rosary, pray for me. Help me to grow in joy and to accept the will of God in this and in all things. Amen.

● • • • • • ● • • • • • ● • • • • • ● • • • • • ● • • • • • ●

Concluding Prayer: I bind these snow-white buds with a petition for the virtue of charity and humbly lay this bouquet at your feet.

The Third Joyful Mystery:
The Birth of Our Lord

All this took place to fulfill what the Lord had said through the prophet: "Behold, the virgin shall be with child and bear a son, and they shall name him Emmanuel," which means "God is with us."
— Matthew 1:22–23

God is with us, and that is the reason for our joy. The Birth of Our Lord is the fulfillment of God's promise. Mary, as I thank God for the blessings he has given to me and to the world, I rejoice in this most perfect gift.

Mary, Queen of the Most Holy Rosary, pray for me. Help me to grow in joy and to accept the will of God in this and in all things. Amen.

Concluding Prayer: I bind these snow-white buds with a petition for the virtue of detachment from the world and humbly lay this bouquet at your feet.

The Fourth Joyful Mystery:
The Presentation in the Temple

Coming forward at that very time, [Anna] gave
thanks to God and spoke about the child to all
who were awaiting the redemption of Jerusalem.
                                    — *Luke 2:38*

God's people had waited so long for the Messiah to come. How they must have rejoiced to hear Anna's witness that their savior had been born into the world. Mary, I thank God today for the ways others have pointed me toward your son.

Mary, Queen of the Most Holy Rosary, pray for me. Help me to grow in joy and to accept the will of God in this and in all things. Amen.

●·····●·····●·····●·····●·····●

Concluding Prayer: I bind these snow-white buds with a petition for the virtue of purity and humbly lay this bouquet at your feet.

The Fifth Joyful Mystery:
The Finding of the Child Jesus in the Temple

*When his parents saw him, they were astonished,
and his mother said to him, "Son, why have you
done this to us? Your father and I have been
looking for you with great anxiety." And he said
to them, "Why were you looking for me? Did you
not know that I must be in my Father's house?"*
— *Luke 2:48–49*

The Finding of the Child Jesus in the Temple reminds us to be thankful when a situation that causes us great anxiety has a joyful outcome. Mary, your son's response to your anxious question confirms his knowledge of God's will for him. I pray today to know and to be thankful for God's will for me.

Mary, Queen of the Most Holy Rosary, pray for me. Help me to grow in joy and to accept the will of God in this and in all things. Amen.

•·····•·····•·····•·····•·····•

Concluding Prayer: I bind these snow-white buds with a petition for the virtue of obedience to the will of God and humbly lay this bouquet at your feet.

Closing Prayer for the Joyful Mysteries
(in Thanksgiving)

Spiritual Communion: My Jesus, I believe that you are present in the most Blessed Sacrament. I love you above all things and I desire to receive you into my soul. Since I cannot now receive you sacramentally, come at least spiritually into my heart. I embrace you as if you were already there and unite myself wholly to you. Never permit me to be separated from you. Amen.

● · · · · · ● · · · · · ● · · · · · ● · · · · · ● · · · · · ●

Concluding Prayer: Sweet Mother Mary, I offer you this spiritual communion to bind my bouquets in a wreath to place upon your brow in thanksgiving for my request, which you in your love have obtained for me.

François Spierre, *The Last Supper, the interior of a classical building with Christ and his apostles seated at a table*, 1660–1681, The Metropolitan Museum of Art, The Elisha Whittelsey Collection, The Elisha Whittelsey Fund, 1951

The Luminous Mysteries

Peace I leave with you; my peace I give to you.
Not as the world gives do I give it to you. Do
not let your hearts be troubled or afraid.
— John 14:27

As we pray the Luminous Mysteries of the Rosary in thanksgiving that the Lord hears our prayers for this special intention, we ponder each mystery with a focus on finding peace within our hearts. We know that the peace given to us by God is a lasting peace that comes through hearing and following his Word.

Opening Prayer for the
Luminous Mysteries
(in Thanksgiving)

Hail, Queen of the Most Holy Rosary, my Mother Mary, hail! At your feet I humbly kneel to offer you a crown of roses, bright yellow buds to remind you of the ministry of your son, each bud recalling to you a holy mystery, each ten bound together with my petition for a particular grace. O Holy Queen, dispenser of God's graces, and mother of all who invoke you! You cannot look upon my gift and fail to see its binding. As you receive my gift, so will you receive my thanksgiving; from your bounty, you have given me the favor I so earnestly and trustingly sought. I did not despair of what I asked of you, and you have truly shown yourself my mother.

_____

_____

_____

_____

_____

_____

The First Luminous Mystery:
The Baptism in the Jordan

Jesus came from Nazareth of Galilee and was baptized in the Jordan by John. On coming up out of the water he saw the heavens being torn open and the Spirit, like a dove, descending upon him.
— Mark 1:9–10

When the Holy Spirit descended upon Jesus in the Jordan, God affirmed that Jesus was his Son who had been sent into the world. Mary, I pray today that I will know the peace that comes from trusting in God.

Mary, Queen of the Most Holy Rosary, pray for me. Help me to grow in peace and to accept the will of God in this and in all things. Amen.

● · · · · · ● · · · · · ● · · · · · ● · · · · · ● · · · · · ●

Concluding Prayer: I bind these bright yellow roses with a petition for the grace of openness to the Holy Spirit and humbly lay this bouquet at your feet.

The Second Luminous Mystery:
The Wedding at Cana

His mother said to the servers,
"Do whatever he tells you."

— *John 2:5*

Your words at the Wedding at Cana, Mary, are not only for the servants; they are for all of us. They also summarize the way you lived your life. I pray that I will know the peace that comes from doing what God asks.

Mary, Queen of the Most Holy Rosary, pray for me. Help me to grow in peace and to accept the will of God in this and in all things. Amen.

•·····•·····•·····•·····•·····•

Concluding Prayer: I bind these bright yellow roses with a petition for the grace of manifestation through faith and humbly lay this bouquet at your feet.

The Third Luminous Mystery:
The Proclamation of the Kingdom of God

Jesus came to Galilee proclaiming the gospel of God: "This is the time of fulfillment. The kingdom of God is at hand. Repent, and believe in the gospel."
— *Mark 1:14–15*

A time of fulfillment is a time for peace and thanksgiving. Mary, help me to look at the circumstances in my life and see the ways God has fulfilled his promises. I pray that I will be grateful for the large and small graces I have received.

Mary, Queen of the Most Holy Rosary, pray for me. Help me to grow in peace and to accept the will of God in this and in all things. Amen.

•·····•·····•·····•·····•·····•

Concluding Prayer: I bind these bright yellow roses with a petition for the grace of trust in God and humbly lay this bouquet at your feet.

The Fourth Luminous Mystery:
The Transfiguration

Jesus took Peter, James, and John his brother, and led them up a high mountain by themselves. And he was transfigured before them; his face shone like the sun and his clothes became white as light.
— Matthew 17:1–2

The Transfiguration was a preview of the glory of God. I pray that I will never miss an opportunity to see God's glory in my daily life. Mary, help me to remember to thank God for all I have been given.

Mary, Queen of the Most Holy Rosary, pray for me. Help me to grow in peace and to accept the will of God in this and in all things. Amen.

● ⋯⋯ ● ⋯⋯ ● ⋯⋯ ● ⋯⋯ ● ⋯⋯ ●

Concluding Prayer: I bind these bright yellow roses with a petition for the grace of desire for holiness and humbly lay this bouquet at your feet.

The Fifth Luminous Mystery:
The Institution of the Eucharist

*While they were eating, Jesus took bread, said
the blessing, broke it, and giving it to his disciples
said, "Take and eat; this is my body." Then he
took a cup, gave thanks, and gave it to them,
saying, "Drink from it, all of you, for this is my
blood of the covenant, which will be shed on
behalf of many for the forgiveness of sins."*
— *Matthew 26:26–28*

The Eucharist is the ultimate way to give thanks to God, fulfilling the command to do this in memory of Jesus. Mary, your son's sacrifice is the promise of God's forgiveness that saves our souls. I pray in thanksgiving for this, the greatest gift.

Mary, Queen of the Most Holy Rosary, pray for me. Help me to grow in peace and to accept the will of God in this and in all things. Amen.

●······●······●······●······●······●

Concluding Prayer: I bind these bright yellow roses with a petition for the grace of adoration of the Eucharist and humbly lay this bouquet at your feet.

Closing Prayer for the
Luminous Mysteries
(in Thanksgiving)

Spiritual Communion: My Jesus, I believe that you are present in the most Blessed Sacrament. I love you above all things and I desire to receive you into my soul. Since I cannot now receive you sacramentally, come at least spiritually into my heart. I embrace you as if you were already there and unite myself wholly to you. Never permit me to be separated from you. Amen.

•·····•·····•·····•·····•·····•

Concluding Prayer: Sweet Mother Mary, I offer you this spiritual communion to bind my bouquets in a wreath to place upon your brow in thanksgiving for my request, which you in your love have obtained for me.

Jacopo Palma the Younger, *The Crucifixion*, The Metropolitan Museum of Art,
Gift of Robert Lehman, 1957

The Sorrowful Mysteries

Whatever you ask for in prayer
with faith, you will receive.
— *Matthew 21:22*

As we pray the Sorrowful Mysteries of the Rosary in thanksgiving that the Lord hears our prayers for this special intention, we ponder each mystery with a focus on strengthening our faith. The strength we need to endure difficult circumstances and trust God despite everything can only come through faith.

Opening Prayer for the
Sorrowful Mysteries
(in Thanksgiving)

Hail, Queen of the Most Holy Rosary, my Mother Mary, hail! At your feet I gratefully kneel to offer you a crown of roses, blood-red roses to remind you of the passion of your divine son, with whom you did so fully partake of its bitterness, each rose recalling to you a holy mystery, each ten bound together with my petition for a particular grace. O Holy Queen, dispenser of God's graces, and mother of all who invoke you! You cannot look upon my gift and fail to see its binding. As you receive my gift, so will you receive my thanksgiving; from your bounty, you have given me the favor I so earnestly and trustingly sought. I did not despair of what I asked of you, and you have truly shown yourself my mother.

_____

_____

_____

_____

_____

The First Sorrowful Mystery:
The Agony in the Garden

He said to them, "My soul is sorrowful even to death. Remain here and keep watch with me."
— Matthew 26:38

Even though he was God, Jesus still experienced sorrow and loneliness. Though the apostles ran away and fell asleep, Jesus stayed awake to pray in his distress. Mary, your son's agony is yours as well. I pray that when I am in distress, I will remember to believe that God is with me.

Mary, Queen of the Most Holy Rosary, pray for me. Help me to grow in faith and to accept the will of God in this and in all things. Amen.

• •

Concluding Prayer: I bind these blood-red roses with a petition for the virtue of resignation to the will of God and humbly lay this bouquet at thy feet.

The Second Sorrowful Mystery:
The Scourging at the Pillar

Pilate, wishing to satisfy the crowd, released Barabbas to them and, after he had Jesus scourged, handed him over to be crucified.

— *Mark 15:15*

Pilate showed his cowardice in giving in to the crowd's demands although he knew Jesus was innocent. As I pray today, Mary, I seek the courage I will need to accept and to be thankful for what God has in store for me.

Mary, Queen of the Most Holy Rosary, pray for me. Help me to grow in faith and to accept the will of God in this and in all things. Amen.

•·····•·····•·····•·····•·····•

Concluding Prayer: I bind these blood-red roses with a petition for the virtue of mortification and humbly lay this bouquet at your feet.

The Third Sorrowful Mystery:
The Crowning with Thorns

*They clothed him in purple and, weaving
a crown of thorns, placed it on him.*

— Mark 15:17

It is difficult to contemplate Jesus being mocked by the Roman soldiers and the crowd. The crown of thorns, an instrument of pain, is the wrong kind of crown for the Prince of Peace. Yet Jesus accepted the pain. Mary, I pray that when I experience pain, my faith will remain strong.

Mary, Queen of the Most Holy Rosary, pray for me. Help me to grow in faith and to accept the will of God in this and in all things. Amen.

•••••••••••••••••••••••••••••

Concluding Prayer: I bind these blood-red roses with a petition for the virtue of humility and humbly lay this bouquet at your feet.

The Fourth Sorrowful Mystery:
The Carrying of the Cross

*When they had mocked him, they stripped
him of the cloak, dressed him in his own
clothes, and led him off to crucify him.*
                                    — Matthew 27:31

As Jesus carried the heavy burden of his cross to the place where he would be crucified, he did not give up in discouragement. I pray that I, too, will endure, even if I don't see a way out of a difficult situation. Mary, as you accompanied your son on the road to Calvary, please stay with me in my time of need.

Mary, Queen of the Most Holy Rosary, pray for me. Help me to grow in faith and to accept the will of God in this and in all things. Amen.

●······●······●······●······●······●

Concluding Prayer: I bind these blood-red roses with a petition for the virtue of patience in adversity and humbly lay this bouquet at your feet.

The Fifth Sorrowful Mystery:
The Crucifixion

When Jesus saw his mother and the disciple there whom he loved, he said to his mother, "Woman, behold, your son." Then he said to the disciple, "Behold, your mother." And from that hour the disciple took her into his home.
— John 19:26–27

Mary, your son gave you to all of us as our heavenly mother. We can come to you like little children seeking comfort and care. I am grateful that God loved the world so much that he not only gave his only Son for our salvation, but also gave us a mother who would help us stay close to him.

Mary, Queen of the Most Holy Rosary, pray for me. Help me to grow in faith and to accept the will of God in this and in all things. Amen.

• •

Concluding Prayer: I bind these blood-red roses with a petition for the virtue of love of our enemies and humbly lay this bouquet at your feet.

Closing Prayer for the
Sorrowful Mysteries
(in Thanksgiving)

Spiritual Communion: My Jesus, I believe that you are present in the most Blessed Sacrament. I love you above all things and I desire to receive you into my soul. Since I cannot now receive you sacramentally, come at least spiritually into my heart. I embrace you as if you were already there and unite myself wholly to you. Never permit me to be separated from you. Amen.

• · · · · · • · · · · · • · · · · · • · · · · · • · · · · · •

Concluding Prayer: Sweet Mother Mary, I offer you this spiritual communion to bind my bouquets in a wreath to place upon your brow in thanksgiving for my request, which you in your love have obtained for me.

François Ragot, *The Assumption of the Virgin*, mid 17th–late 17th century,
The Metropolitan Museum of Art, The Elisha Whittelsey Collection,
The Elisha Whittelsey Fund, 1951

The Glorious Mysteries

Give thanks to the Lord, invoke his name; make known among the peoples his deeds. Sing praise, play music; proclaim all his wondrous deeds. Glory in his holy name; rejoice, O hearts that seek the Lord.
— *1 Chronicles 16:8–10*

As we pray the Glorious Mysteries of the Rosary in thanksgiving that the Lord hears our prayers for this special intention, we ponder each mystery with a focus on gratitude. Thanksgiving is the expression of our joy in knowing that God truly loves us and is at work in our lives.

Opening Prayer for the Glorious Mysteries (in Thanksgiving)

Hail, Queen of the Most Holy Rosary, my Mother Mary, hail! At your feet I gratefully kneel to offer you a crown of roses, full-blown white roses, tinged with the red of the passion, to remind you of your glories, fruits of the sufferings of your son and you, each rose recalling to you a holy mystery, each ten bound together with my petition for a particular grace. O Holy Queen, dispenser of God's graces, and mother of all who invoke you! You cannot look upon my gift and fail to see its binding. As you receive my gift, so will you receive my thanksgiving; from your bounty you have given me the favor I so earnestly and trustingly sought. I did not despair of what I asked of you, and you have truly shown yourself my mother.

_____

_____

_____

_____

The First Glorious Mystery:
The Resurrection

*He is not here, for he has been raised just as he
said. Come and see the place where he lay.*
— Matthew 28:6

J esus' resurrection confirms for us that God keeps his
promises. It also reminds us of God's power over all
things — even death. As a witness to Jesus' death and
Resurrection, Mary, you saw those promises fulfilled before your eyes. I come to you today with thanksgiving in
my heart for the many ways God has worked, and will
work, in my life.

Mary, Queen of the Most Holy Rosary, pray for me.
Help me to grow in gratitude and to accept the will of
God in this and in all things. Amen.

•·····•·····•·····•·····•·····•

Concluding Prayer: I bind these full-blown roses with a
petition for the virtue of faith and humbly lay this bouquet at your feet.

The Second Glorious Mystery:
The Ascension of Our Lord

As he blessed them he parted from them
and was taken up to heaven.

— Luke 24:51

The ascension of Jesus into heaven is an end and a beginning. Jesus blessed his followers before taking his place with the Father. God's blessing is a promise we can count on. Mary, help me to always be grateful for the ways God has blessed me.

Mary, Queen of the Most Holy Rosary, pray for me. Help me to grow in gratitude and to accept the will of God in this and in all things. Amen.

⁕⁕⁕⁕⁕

Concluding Prayer: I bind these full-blown roses with a petition for the virtue of hope and humbly lay this bouquet at your feet.

The Third Glorious Mystery:
The Descent of the Holy Spirit

Then there appeared to them tongues as of fire, which parted and came to rest on each one of them. And they were all filled with the holy Spirit and began to speak in different tongues, as the Spirit enabled them to proclaim.

— *Acts 2:3–4*

When the Holy Spirit came upon the Apostles, they were transformed, able to speak many languages to reach multitudes over all the earth. Mary, you witnessed how the Apostles were strengthened by the gifts of the Holy Spirit. As I pray today, help me to always thank God for the gifts I have received through the Holy Spirit and to use those gifts to help spread God's love in the world.

Mary, Queen of the Most Holy Rosary, pray for me. Help me to grow in gratitude and to accept the will of God in this and in all things. Amen.

•·····•·····•·····•·····•·····•

Concluding Prayer: I bind these full-blown roses with a petition for the virtue of charity and humbly lay this bouquet at your feet.

The Fourth Glorious Mystery:
The Assumption of Our Lady into Heaven

She already shares in the glory of her
Son's Resurrection, anticipating the
resurrection of all members of his Body.
— Catechism of the Catholic Church, 974

Mary, your assumption into heaven completed your life on earth, but you have let us know in many ways that you are still present in our lives, always pointing us toward your son. I pray today in gratitude that you stand with me and urge me to keep praying. I am thankful that Christ has shared his mother with the world.

Mary, Queen of the Most Holy Rosary, pray for me. Help me to grow in gratitude and to accept the will of God in this and in all things. Amen.

●·····●·····●·····●·····●·····●

Concluding Prayer: I bind these full-blown roses with a petition for the virtue of union with Christ and humbly lay this bouquet at your feet.

The Fifth Glorious Mystery:
The Coronation of the Blessed Virgin Mary

*A great sign appeared in the sky, a woman clothed
with the sun, with the moon under her feet,
and on her head a crown of twelve stars.*
— *Revelation 12:1*

Though you are the queen of heaven, Mary, you have shown over and over that you care for God's people here on earth. I am thankful today that I can turn to you with the cares and burdens I carry, knowing you are with me, encouraging me to trust in God.

Mary, Queen of the Most Holy Rosary, pray for me. Help me to grow in gratitude and to accept the will of God in this and in all things. Amen.

•·····•·····•·····•·····•·····•

Concluding Prayer: I bind these full-blown roses with a petition for the virtue of union with you and humbly lay this bouquet at your feet.

Closing Prayer for the
Glorious Mysteries
(in Thanksgiving)

Spiritual Communion: My Jesus, I believe that you are present in the most Blessed Sacrament. I love you above all things and I desire to receive you into my soul. Since I cannot now receive you sacramentally, come at least spiritually into my heart. I embrace you as if you were already there and unite myself wholly to you. Never permit me to be separated from you. Amen.

●·····●·····●·····●·····●·····●

Concluding Prayer: Sweet Mother Mary, I offer you this spiritual communion to bind my bouquets in a wreath to place upon your brow in thanksgiving for my request, which you in your love have obtained for me.

How to Pray the Rosary

The Order of the Prayers of the Rosary

Begin at the crucifix. Make the Sign of the Cross, then pray the Apostles' Creed.

Pray one Our Father (on the large bead).

Pray three Hail Marys (on the small beads).

Pray the Glory Be (in the space between the small bead and the large bead).

Announce the first mystery, then pray an Our Father (on the large bead).

Pray the first decade of the Rosary, ten Hail Marys (on the small beads), while meditating on the mystery.

Pray the Glory Be and the Fatima Prayer.

Announce the next mystery, followed by an Our Father.

For each decade, pray ten Hail Marys while meditating on the mystery.

Pray the Glory Be and the Fatima Prayer.

After the five decades are completed, pray the Hail, Holy Queen (on the medal or centerpiece of the Rosary) and the concluding Rosary Prayer.

The Prayers of the Rosary

Apostles' Creed
I believe in God,
the Father almighty,
Creator of heaven and earth,
and in Jesus Christ, his only Son, our Lord,
who was conceived by the Holy Spirit,
born of the Virgin Mary,
suffered under Pontius Pilate,
was crucified, died and was buried;
he descended into hell;
on the third day he rose again from the dead;
he ascended into heaven,
and is seated at the right hand of God the Father
    almighty;
from there he will come to judge the living and the dead.

I believe in the Holy Spirit,
the holy catholic Church,
the communion of saints,
the forgiveness of sins,
the resurrection of the body,
and life everlasting.

Amen.

Our Father

Our Father, who art in heaven, hallowed be thy name; thy kingdom come; thy will be done on earth as it is in heaven. Give us this day our daily bread; and forgive us our trespasses as we forgive those who trespass against us; and lead us not into temptation, but deliver us from evil. Amen.

•·····•·····•·····•·····•·····•

Hail Mary

Hail Mary, full of grace. The Lord is with thee; blessed art thou among women, and blessed is the fruit of thy womb, Jesus. Holy Mary, Mother of God, pray for us sinners, now and at the hour of our death. Amen.

•·····•·····•·····•·····•·····•

Glory Be (The Doxology)

Glory be to the Father, and to the Son, and to the Holy Spirit; as it was in the beginning, is now, and ever shall be, world without end. Amen.

•·····•·····•·····•·····•·····•

Fatima Prayer

O my Jesus, forgive us our sins; save us from the fires of hell. Lead all souls to heaven, especially those who have most need of your mercy.

Hail, Holy Queen

Hail, holy Queen, mother of mercy, our life, our sweetness, and our hope. To you do we cry, poor banished children of Eve; to you do we send up our sighs, mourning, and weeping in this valley of tears. Turn, then, most gracious advocate, your eyes of mercy toward us; and after this, our exile, show unto us the blessed fruit of your womb, Jesus. O clement, O loving, O sweet Virgin Mary.

V. Pray for us, O Holy Mother of God
R. That we may be made worthy of the promises of Christ.

●·····●·····●·····●·····●·····●

Concluding Rosary Prayer

O God, whose only begotten Son, by his life, death, and resurrection, has purchased for us the rewards of eternal life, grant, we beseech thee, that meditating upon these mysteries of the Most Holy Rosary of the Blessed Virgin Mary, we may imitate what they contain and obtain what they promise, through the same Christ Our Lord. Amen.

The Fifteen Promises
of the Rosary

According to pious tradition, the fifteenth-century Dominican friar Alanus de Rupe experienced a private revelation from the Blessed Virgin Mary, who offered these fifteen promises to those who pray the Rosary devoutly:

1. Those who faithfully serve me by the recitation of the Rosary shall receive signal graces.
2. I promise my special protection and the greatest graces to all those who shall recite the Rosary.
3. The Rosary shall be a powerful armor against hell. It will destroy vice, decrease sin, and defeat heresies.
4. The recitation of the Rosary will cause virtue and good works to flourish. It will obtain for souls the abundant mercy of God. It will withdraw the hearts of men from the love of the world and its vanities, and will lift them to the desire of eternal things. Oh, that souls would sanctify themselves by this means.

5. The soul which recommends itself to me by the recitation of the Rosary shall not perish.

6. Those who recite my Rosary devoutly, applying themselves to the consideration of its sacred mysteries, shall never be conquered by misfortune. In his justice, God will not chastise them; nor shall they perish by an unprovided death, that is, be unprepared for heaven. Sinners shall convert. The just shall persevere in grace and become worthy of eternal life.

7. Those who have a true devotion to the Rosary shall not die without the sacraments of the Church.

8. Those who faithfully recite the Rosary shall have, during their life and at their death, the light of God and the plenitude of his graces. At the moment of death, they shall participate in the merits of the saints in paradise.

9. I shall deliver from purgatory those who have been devoted to the Rosary.

10. The faithful children of the Rosary shall merit a high degree of glory in heaven.

11. By the recitation of the Rosary you shall obtain all that you ask of me.

12. Those who propagate the holy Rosary shall be aided by me in their necessities.

13. I have obtained from my divine son that all the advocates of the Rosary shall have for intercessors the entire celestial court during their life and at the hour of their death.

14. All who recite the Rosary are my beloved children and the brothers and sisters of my only son, Jesus Christ.

15. Devotion for my Rosary is a great sign of predestination.

Artwork

Our Lady of the Rosary at Pompeii.

Claude Mellan, *Annunciation*, 1666, The Metropolitan Museum of Art, Harris Brisbane Dick Fund, 1953.

Paul Gleditsch, *The Baptism of Christ; Saint John the Baptist at right and Christ at left with his hands held together, the Holy Dove above, angels in the background, after Reni*, ca. 1815–72, The Metropolitan Museum of Art, Harris Brisbane Dick Fund, 1947.

Benoit Thiboust, *Agony in the Garden*, 1680–1719, The Metropolitan Museum of Art, The Elisha Whittelsey Collection, The Elisha Whittelsey Fund, 1951.

Follower of Francesco Fontebasso, *The Resurrection*, 18th century, National Gallery of Art, Gift of Dr. and Mrs. Malcolm W. Bick.

Nicolas Mignard, *The Visitation*, c. 1649, The Metropolitan Museum of Art, Gift of Matthieu de Bayser, 2010.

François Spierre, *The Last Supper, the interior of a classical building with Christ and his apostles seated at a table*, 1660–1681, The Metropolitan Museum of Art, The Elisha Whittelsey Collection, The Elisha Whittelsey Fund, 1951.

Jacopo Palma the Younger, *The Crucifixion*, The Met Museum, Gift of Robert Lehman, 1957.

François Ragot, *The Assumption of the Virgin*, mid 17th–late 17th century, The Metropolitan Museum of Art, The Elisha Whittelsey Collection, The Elisha Whittelsey Fund, 1951.